WEST NORTHAMPTONSHIRE COUNCIL	
60000549226	
Askews & Holts	
WR	

MAGICAL MUSEUMS

ADVENTURES IN TECHNOLOGY

Ben Hubbard and Max Rambaldi

WAYLAND

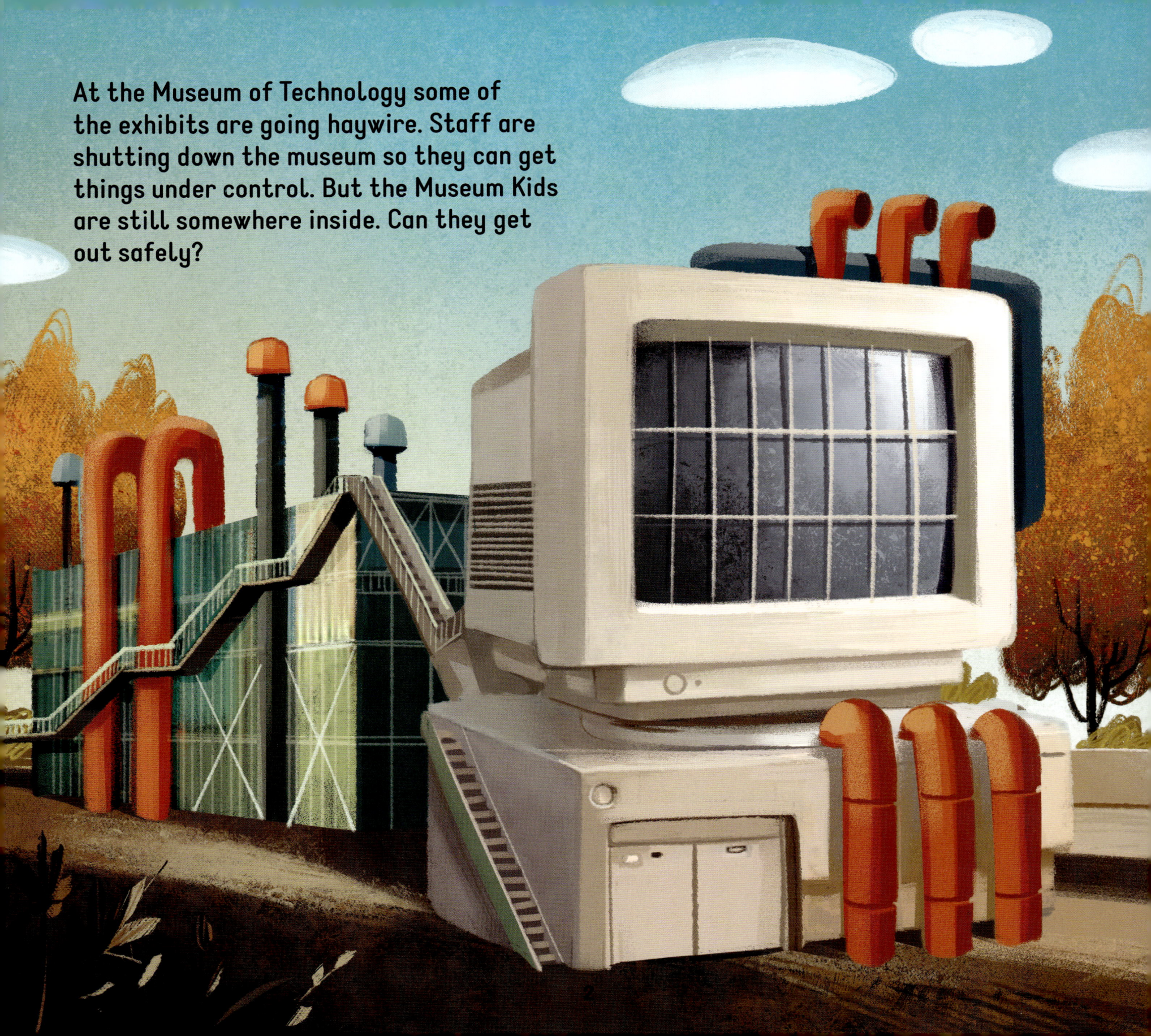

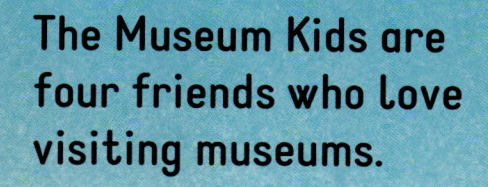

The Museum Kids are four friends who love visiting museums.

Min is a tech wizard who lives for machines, screens and electronics. Able to build almost any gadget from scratch, Min is super-serious and sometimes a little shy.

Aga is a science and space lover with energy to spare. She is brave, confident and likes to be a leader! Planes and spaceships are her favourite subjects.

Hung is an outdoor adventurer who is crazy about animals and the environment. He is usually bodyboarding, studying sea creatures or cracking jokes.

Bako is a keen reader and, like his friends, he loves to learn. His favourite subjects are geology and history. Sometimes it's hard to pry his nose from his latest book.

Museum staff are rushing visitors out as lights flash and sirens wail around them. But the Museum Kids aren't in a hurry. Waiting by the lifts, Aga complains she didn't see the flying car and Min is texting on her smartwatch. Hung is messing about with Bako as they step into the lift. But is this really a lift?

"This is my favourite museum. I don't want to leave!"

The lift lands in the Olduvai Gorge in Tanzania, Africa, around 1.8 million years ago. Towering above the Museum Kids are giants in fur clothes using the first stone tools! "What's going on?" Min gasps. "Uh, oh," says Akira. "I think the lift has crossed wires with the museum's shrinking machine. We've all shrunk. These people are *Homo habilis*. They aren't actually giants!"

Stone tool

To make a stone tool, an early human used a hard rock to chip pieces off one side of another rock. This made a sharp cutting edge that could be used to chop branches from trees, cut meat from animals or smash bones to get at the marrow inside.

The lift takes off again and lands in Mesopotamia (modern-day Iraq) where the wheel has just been invented. But the kids are still small and have to hide in wet clay. Now they are stuck fast. Bako, Aga and Hung start shouting to Akira for help.

Potter's wheel
Most experts think that the Mesopotamians invented the wheel in around 3,500 BCE. A stone or clay disk with a circular hole, the wheel was used to make pottery. The potter turned the wheel by hand, shaping wet clay into pots and other objects.

Chariots

The first-known chariots were used in Mesopotamia in around 3,000 BCE. They were heavy vehicles with four wooden wheels. Towed by oxen or donkeys, the chariots could fit one or two spearmen, as well as the driver.

How does a wheel work?

On a vehicle, wheels are connected to a pole, called an axle. The axle is then attached to the vehicle's body. When the wheels move, so does the axle, and therefore the vehicle too.

Axle

Just as things look desperate, the lift comes to the rescue. Two arms spring out and pull the gang free. Now back into the lift for take-off!

Over here, quick!

The lift is awesome. It never lets you down!

The lift has landed on an ancient Greek trireme. It's so windy that the lift has attached itself to a mast. Bako sees an astrolabe being used on deck below. Hung and Aga start messing about on a rope. But Min spies trouble: a sea hawk has spotted them. Akira and the lift to the rescue!

Ancient astrolabe

In around 200 BCE, the ancient Greeks invented the astrolabe to navigate at sea. The astrolabe worked by measuring the angles between objects in the sky, such as the stars. This helped ships work out their position. Later, Muslim astronomers made further improvements to astrolabes.

Shall I sell the sailors my smartphone? It has a compass.

It wouldn't be much good to them after the battery loses power!

Chinese compass

The first compass was invented in China in the 3rd century BCE. Over the next thousand years, Chinese people developed small compasses used by sailors to work out which direction they were going. The compass's iron needle was magnetised to always point north.

Sailor's sextant

The sextant became a sailor's main tool for navigation after it was developed in the early 1730s. By looking through the sextant's eyepiece, a sailor could measure the height of the Sun in relation to the horizon. This information, together with the correct time, was then used with sea charts to determine the ship's location.

The next stop is Germany where the printing press is the latest, greatest invention. But the lift has broken down – and it's stranded on the press! The kids have only minutes to save it before it's crushed. Aga tells Hung to give Min a leg up, while Bako looks for a lift manual on his tablet. If the kids can't fix the lift, they'll be stuck in 1439!

Don't worry. Min can fix anything!

Gutenberg's press

When Johannes Gutenberg invented the first mechanised printing press in 1439, it was a technological breakthrough. Before this, books would be copied by hand. Now, using trays of movable type, Gutenberg's press could print 250 pages an hour. This led to mass-produced books and a new age of information.

Oldest book
The oldest surviving book printed with movable type is the Korean *Jikji*. It was created in 1377.

What is movable type?
Gutenberg made metal moulds of letters and symbols. These were arranged in a tray to make words and sentences. Once the text was ready, the printer added ink to the letters and pressed paper onto them to print a page.

Just as the press starts crushing the lift, it vanishes into thin air. Min fixed it. Phew!

The lift has landed in 1888 on the back of the world's first car. But the car has been taken on the world's first joyride by the inventor's wife, Bertha. This is great fun! Aga tries to stop Akira falling off as Bako explains the car is called the Motorwagen.

People look amazed! I guess they haven't seen a car before.

I know. They haven't even noticed us!

The Motorwagen

German inventor Karl Benz dreamed of building a 'horseless carriage' that didn't need rails or horses to work. By 1885, he had designed an internal combustion engine and placed it in a steel frame with three wheels. This was the world's first car! However, people complained Benz's Motorwagen was too loud and Benz worried that no one would buy it. His wife Bertha decided to make a 180-km trip in the car to show people it could do long journeys. Soon orders rolled in.

Model T

While Karl Benz invented the car, American businessman Henry Ford made an affordable version. Instead of a team of workers building each car, Ford invented the assembly line in 1913. Each worker would add a single part as Ford's Model T car slid past. Various versions of the Model T were added until the last one rolled off the production line in 1927.

What is an internal combustion engine?

An internal combustion engine is powered by the burning of fuel. This builds up pressure in a cylinder, which pushes a rod that is attached to a wheel. The rod pushes the wheel and makes it turn. The spinning wheel is attached to the car's other four wheels by a belt, or chain.

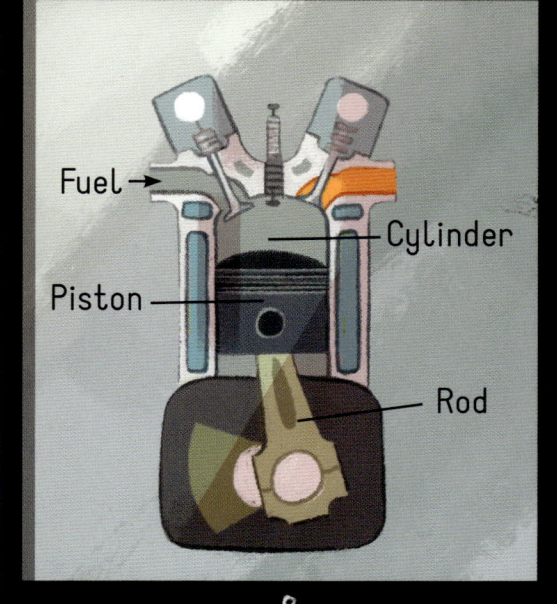

Fuel
Cylinder
Piston
Rod

The lift has landed in the museum's hall of light bulbs. Before light bulbs were invented, people used candles and oil lamps to light their homes. But the museum hall is dark and creepy. There are weird scuttling and scratching sounds coming from the shadows. The kids hold their breath.

Swan's light

Between 1850 and 1860, British physicist Joseph Swan created a 'light bulb' by enclosing a paper filament in a glass bulb. The filament glowed brightly when electricity was passed through it.

Davy's light

In 1809, British scientist Humphrey Davy invented an electric 'arc light'. This worked by passing electricity between two charcoal strips, thus creating a bright 'arc' of light.

What's in a light bulb?

In an incandescent light bulb, an electric current flows into a thin wire called a filament, which makes it glow and give out light and heat. In a light-emitting diode (LED) light, strips of LEDs replace the incandescent filament. These LEDs glow when a current passes through them, but they do not heat up.

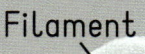
Filament

LEDs

Edison's light

In 1878, American inventor Thomas Edison developed his own light bulb. This worked by passing electricity through a carbon filament. The result was the long-lasting incandescent light bulb.

Holonyak's light

In 1962, American engineer Nick Holonyak invented the light-emitting diode (LED). This led to an LED light bulb that was more energy-efficient and longer-lasting than incandescent light bulbs.

It's really eerie in here.

What do you think is making that scratching noise?

It could be coming from the light bulbs? Or it could be a ghost!

No, it's not a ghost. It's just Crabbie!

The lift lands in 1876, just as the first call is made on a brand new invention – the telephone. But the kids have been seen! Hung, Aga and Min quickly find a hiding spot, but Bako just stands and stares. Luckily, the amazed assistant is called out of the room. They are safe, for the moment.

First phone call

Inventor Alexander Graham Bell was convinced the sound of a human voice could be sent over a wire. In 1876, he received a patent for his design. A few days later, he made the first phone call across a wire to his assistant in the next room. He said: "Mr Watson, come here. I need you."

Rotary phones

Early telephone users had to call a central telephone exchange to connect to another user. But in around 1904, rotary phones came into use. These allowed a user to call another user directly.

Mobile phones

The first mobile phones appeared in the 1970s. These brick-sized devices were over 23 cm long and weighed 1.1 kg! The mobile phone as we know it today did not come into widespread use until the 1990s. The first text message was sent in 1992. It read 'Merry Christmas'.

Televisions for home

In the 1930s, new 'electronic' televisions replaced the mechanical versions. These televisions used an electron gun called a cathode ray tube. The gun fired a stream of electrons to create images on a brightly lit screen.

Colour television

In the 1950s, colour TV broadcasts began in the United States. In 1954, the Tournament of Roses parade became the first colour broadcast.

How does TV work?

A television camera captures light and sound from the subject it is filming and codes the information into an electrical signal. The electrical signal is then sent to a television, which converts it into beams of red, green and blue. The beams are shot at pixels on the television's screen, which recreate the original subject.

The next stop is an American home in 1981. The family are busy with their new home computer. That's good because the pets have taken an interest in the Museum Kids! Min and Hung are having trouble with the cat while the dog is having a sniff at Bako and Aga. They'll have to get back in the lift before they're eaten – or the family notices.

"This cat is stopping me seeing the exhibits!"

"My phone has more computing power than that whole laptop!"

Personal computer

American company IBM's 1981 Personal Computer (PC) launched a computing revolution. In the 1940s, the first computers filled entire rooms and used massive amounts of power to make simple calculations. But the invention of microchips meant computers could be much smaller, small enough for some families to buy one for home use.

The first laptop

Following closely on the heels of the first PC was the first laptop, launched by Japan's Seiko company in 1981. The Epson HX-20's screen could display around four lines of type and also had a thin roll of paper for printing.

The first tablet

Released in 1989, the GRiDPad was the first commercially successful tablet computer. It weighed 2 kg and came with a stylus to write directly onto its green screen. The tablet also came with handwriting-recognition software.

Internet smartphone

Within 10 years of the first tablet, the first Internet-ready smartphone was released. The 1996 Nokia 9000 could send faxes and emails and browse the web. The 1999 Ericsson R380 had many modern smartphone features, but the BlackBerry 5810 became the top seller when it was released in 2002.

Nokia 9000 Ericsson R380 BlackBerry 5810

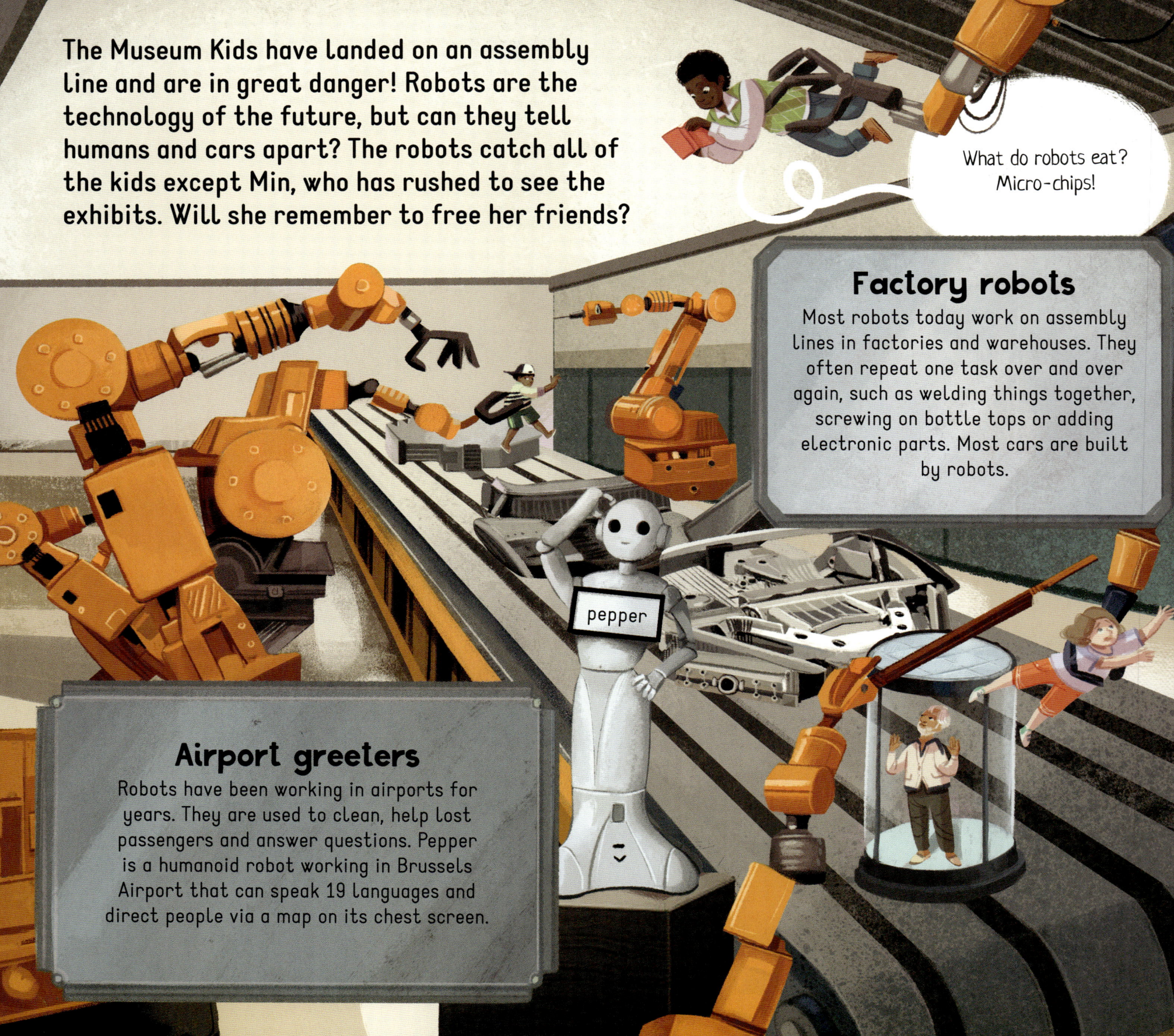

Robot dogs

Not all recent robots are designed to look like humans. Launched in 2020, Spot is a robotic dog with a mechanical arm and cameras attached. This helps Spot open doors, pick up objects, greet visitors and run, jump and play.

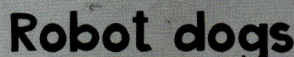
Spot, robotic dog

Human-like face

Ameca is a robot with realistic human expressions. Ameca can blink, smile and look amazed just as if it were human. However, Ameca does not have artificial intelligence (AI), like Pepper and Spot, which would allow it to make its own decisions.

At the last minute, Min notices her friends are about to be squeezed like toothpaste tubes. She hits the factory's off switch. They all rush back into the lift for take-off!

The Museum Kids land safe, sound and un-squeezed at their last stop: the hall of future technology. On the way, something amazing has happened. The kids are all back to being full-sized. But they are so excited by the exhibits, they barely notice. Aga finally sees a flying car, while Hung and Bako try on some smart clothes. Min doesn't want to leave!

Smart clothes

Smart clothes are predicted to have a big role in the wearable technology of the future. Already available are smart T-shirts that record fitness activity and smart pyjamas that release infrared light to soothe sore muscles.

Flying cars

Getting a ride to work or school in a flying car could be possible in the near future. These cars are likely to look like small helicopters, with rotors instead of wings. This will allow them to move forwards and also hover. However, it is unclear what traffic rules would apply to flying cars.

Body nanobots

Many experts think nanobots will be used by doctors in the future. These robots are so small that they can enter the human bloodstream (as seen here). They could also enter our brains and connect us directly to the Internet.

It says here that doctors may use nanobots to check for disease inside us.

I think we had better stop the tour while we are a normal size! But come back to the lobby with me for one last thing before you go.

MUSEUM OF TECHNOLOGY QUIZ

Well guys, what did you think? I bet you're keen to get to the next museum. But first, there is a quiz about the Museum of Technology. Only a good score will unlock the correct door and send you on your way. Good luck!

1. What did *Homo habilis* use the first stone tools for?
   a) To chisel artworks onto rocks
   b) To smash bones and get the marrow
   c) As a juggling tool to entertain others

2. What was the wheel first used for?
   a) To make pottery
   b) To make chariots
   c) To make cars

3. What does the Earth's magnetic field do to a compass needle?
   a) Makes it point south
   b) Makes it point north
   c) Makes it point west

4. How many pages could Gutenberg's printing press print per hour?
   a) 2,500
   b) 25
   c) 250

5. How far did Bertha Benz drive in 1888?
a) 180 km
b) 10 km
c) 50 km

6. Who invented the incandescent light bulb?
a) Thomas Edison
b) Joseph Swan
c) Humphry Davy

7. What did the first laptop include?
a) An inbuilt printer
b) Foldable legs
c) A cassette player

8. In which year was the first personal computer (PC) for homes launched?
a) 1991
b) 1971
c) 1981

How did you do? If you got 4 out 8 questions correct, then well done! The door to the next museum has opened! If you got 3 or fewer questions correct, then the door leading back into this museum has opened. Start at the beginning and go back through!

Check your answers on page 30.

As the kids leave the Museum of Technology, they look at each other and smile. What a wild ride! Magical is the only way to describe it. But their mission isn't finished yet. There are several more magical museums to visit. Check out the kids on their next adventure at a library or bookshop near you.

Answers (pages 28–29)
1. b; 2. a; 3. b; 4. c; 5. a; 6. a; 7. a; 8. c.

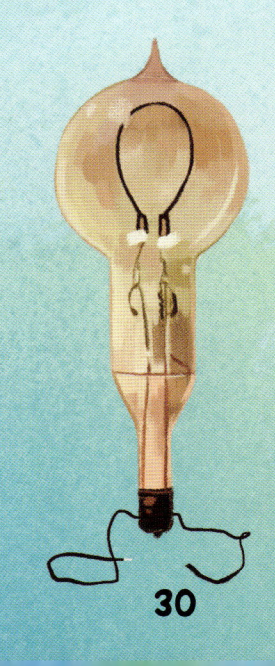

GLOSSARY

artificial intelligence (AI) a computer built to copy human intelligence and behaviour as much as possible

assembly line workers (and machines) along a moving line in a factory. As a product or machine passes along the line, each worker or machine adds a part or performs another job

astronomer someone who studies stars, planets, the Moon and other objects in space

broadcast to send out programmes on radio or television

charcoal a black material made by burning wood very slowly

compass a device with a needle that shows where north is

Earth's magnetic field the pulling force of magnetism surrounding Earth, which has a ball of magnetic iron at its core

electron a very small piece of an atom, the basic building block of everything

exchange a central office in which phone lines are connected. An automatic exchange works without needing people to connect one caller to another

geology the study of Earth and what it is made of

gorge a deep, narrow valley

hover to hang in one place while flying in the air

humanoid looking and acting like a human

incandescent something that produces a bright light when heated

infrared electromagnet waves that cannot be seen

magnetised when a magnet is rubbed along a metal such as iron, from end to end, so that it becomes magnetic and interacts with Earth's magnetic field

manual an instruction booklet on how to use something, such as a machine

marrow soft tissue inside bones where blood cells are made

mass-produced goods made in large numbers, usually in factories using machines

mast a tall pole on a ship which supports the sails

patent the right to be the only person or organisation who can make, use or sell an invention or product

pixel a tiny square of colour on a computer, television or phone screen

printing press a machine that produces printed copies of something, such as a book, using ink and type

rotary phone a 20th century landline phone that uses a number dial instead of buttons

smart clothes clothes with sensors in the fabric to gather information about the wearer and react to it

trireme a long warship powered by oars and sails and used by the ancient Greeks

ventriloquist's dummy a puppet operated by a person to make it look as if the puppet speaks

INDEX

assembly lines 15, 24
astrolabes 10

Baird, John Logie 20
Bell, Alexander Graham 18
Benz, Karl 14–15
    Motorwagen 14

cars 14–15, 24
    flying cars 4, 26–27
chariots 9
Chinese, ancient 11
clothes, smart 26–27
compasses 10–11
computers 22–23

Davy, Humphrey 16

Edison, Thomas 17

Ford, Henry 15
    Model T 15

Greeks, ancient 10
Gutenberg, Johannes 12–13

Holonyak, Nick 17
Homo erectus 7
Homo habilis 6–7
humans, early 6–7

light bulbs 16–17

Mesopotamians 8–9

nanobots 27
navigation 10–11

Olduvai Gorge 6–7

potter's wheels 8
pottery 8
printing 12–13
printing presses 12–13

robots 24–25, 27

sextants 11
smartphones 10, 22–23
Swan, Joseph 16

telephones 18–19
televisions 20–21
tools, stone 6–7
triremes 10–11

wheels 8–9, 15

First published in Great Britain in 2024 by Wayland
Copyright © Hodder and Stoughton, 2024
All rights reserved

Editor: Sarah Peutrill
Designer: Lisa Peacock

HB ISBN : 978 1 5263 2318 7
PB ISBN: 978 1 5263 2319 4

Printed and bound in China

Wayland, an imprint of
Hachette Children's Group
Part of Hodder and Stoughton
Carmelite House
50 Victoria Embankment
London EC4Y 0DZ
An Hachette UK Company

www.hachette.co.uk
www.hachettechildrens.co.uk